D1403794

Medieval
World

KNIGHTS
AND CHIVALRY

KATHY ELGIN

A⁺
Smart Apple Media

First published in the UK by Franklin Watts
96 Leonard Street, London EC2A 4XD

Produced by Arcturus Publishing Ltd.
26/27 Bickels Yard, 151-153 Bermondsey Street, London SE1 3HA
Copyright © 2004 Arcturus Publishing Ltd.

Series concept: Alex Woolf
Editor: Clare Weaver
Designer: Chris Halls, Mind's Eye Design Ltd., Lewes
Illustrator: Peter Dennis
Picture researcher: Glass Onion Pictures

Published in the United States by Smart Apple Media
2140 Howard Drive West, North Mankato, MN 56003

U.S. publication copyright © 2005 Smart Apple Media
International copyright reserved. No part of this book may be reproduced in
any form without written permission from the publisher.
Printed and bound in Italy

Library of Congress Control Number: 2004104268

ISBN 1-58340-568-2

9 8 7 6 5 4 3 2 1

Picture Acknowledgements: The Art Archive/Biblioteca Nazionale Marciana
Venice/Dagli Orti (A) 8, /Bibliothèque Nationale Paris 20, 21, /Bibliothèque Nationale
Paris/Dagli Orti (A) 14, /Bibliothèque Nationale Paris/HarperCollins Publishers 18, 28,
/Bodleian Library Oxford 26 (Auct D inf. 2 11 folio 44v), /British Library 23, /College of
Arms/John Webb 10, /Musée Condé Chantilly/Dagli Orti 15, /Musée des Beaux Arts
Orleans/Dagli Orti (A) 13, /Musée de la Tapisserie Bayeux/Dagli Orti 5, /University
Library Heidelberg/Dagli Orti 9, /Victoria and Albert Museum London/Eileen Tweedy 11;
Bridgeman Art Library/British Museum London 4, /Birmingham Museums and Art
Gallery 29, /Sheffield Galleries and Museums Trust 6; British Library 24 (MS 42130 f82),
27; Royal Armouries 16.

CONTENTS

THE FIRST KNIGHTS

Death of a Hero

The following lines, written in the 11th century, vividly portray the loyalty of a vassal to his lord, even in death:

"Mind must be the firmer, heart the more fierce.
Courage the greater, as our strength diminishes.
Here lies our leader, dead,
A heroic man in the dust.
He who longs to escape will lament forever.
I am old. I will not go from here,
But I mean to lie by the side of my lord,
Lie in the dust with the man I loved so dearly."

(From The Battle of Maldon, *11th century)*

Knighthood grew out of a system known as feudalism, in which a king or lord gave land or property to an individual, his "vassal," in exchange for military service. The vassal swore loyalty to his lord and agreed to fight for him when necessary. In return he received his lord's protection.

Since the collapse of the Roman empire in the fifth century A.D., Europe had existed in a state of almost continual warfare between rival states. Soldiering was a way of life for most men, and it was a brutal business, with bands of armed men roaming the countryside.

Feudalism, however, valued the virtues of loyalty and service to a leader, and gradually a new code of military behavior emerged. Instead of just attacking and pillaging at random, men began to see themselves as united in fighting for a purpose. They took pride in putting their military skills at the service of their lord. This attitude was the beginning of knighthood. It soon spread throughout Europe, arriving in England with the Normans when they conquered the country in 1066. Allegiance to a lord was already at the heart of Anglo-Saxon society, and this new, refined concept of knighthood soon took root.

This sixth-century mosaic shows a Vandal, one of the earliest mounted soldiers.

HIC WILLELM·DVX ALLOQVITVR·SV I·

The famous Bayeux Tapestry records how the new cavalry tactics of William of Normandy and his knights surprised the English at the Battle of Hastings.

The Normans built a network of castles throughout England to help them govern each area, and it was in these great households that the tradition of knighthood became established. As well as physical strength and courage, knighthood demanded obedience, endurance, and a serious and careful approach to life—the early knights aimed to embody Christian virtues. Because they all shared the same ideals, knights came to see themselves not just as English or French but as members of a special international brotherhood. Only the son of a knight could become a knight himself.

Although military life remained at the heart of knighthood, there was a peacetime role as well, as the knight served his lord as escort and companion and in general household duties. With the cult of chivalry during the 13th and 14th centuries (see pages 8 and 9), the knight emerged as the romantic figure people recognize today.

Charlemagne

Charlemagne, King of the Franks from 768 to 814 and Holy Roman Emperor from 800 to 814, was a great warrior who fought constantly to spread Christianity throughout Europe but who also cared about culture, art, and music. Although he lived 300 years before the medieval period, Charlemagne embodied all the knightly virtues. Many of the epic poems and songs that celebrated his triumphs were revived by medieval knights as inspiration for their own exploits.

ORDERS OF KNIGHTHOOD

The Order of the Garter
Edward III intended to found an Order of the Round Table, inspired by King Arthur. In the end he settled for the Order of the Garter. This was composed of 25 knights, all of whom had successfully fought with him against the French at the Battle of Crécy in 1346, and 25 priests who prayed for them in the Order's chapel at Windsor. The Order also paid for the upkeep of 25 poor knights. The Order gained its name from an incident at court, when a lady lost her garter during a lively dance. The king picked it up and fastened it to his own leg. Everyone was shocked, but the king said, "Evil be to him who evil thinks" (*Honi soit qui mal y pense*), which became the Order's motto.

Edward III awards the Order of the Garter to his son, Edward, the Black Prince, who had fought bravely at the Battle of Crécy.

Most knights belonged to an association known as an Order. They swore oaths of loyalty to the Order and its Grand Master, and wore a sash or a badge to identify themselves. The earliest Orders were founded by the Church. The most famous of these were the Knights Templar and the Hospitalers, or Knights of St. John.

Both of these Orders were formed during the Crusades, a series of wars between the 11th and 13th centuries in which European Christian armies attempted to conquer the Holy Land, an area of the Middle East ruled by Muslims (see pages 22 and 23). The Knights Templar were founded to protect Christian pilgrims in the Holy Land, while the Hospitalers cared for sick pilgrims in Jerusalem.

Both Orders became expert fighting forces. "They are milder than lambs and fiercer than lions. They combine the

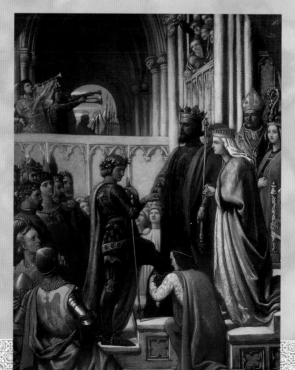

meekness of monks with the fighting courage of knights so completely that I do not know whether to call them knights or contemplatives." This was how Bernard of Clairvaux described the Knights Templar. The Order had more than 20,000 knights and became very rich and powerful.

The Knights Hospitaler were easily recognized by the black cross on their surcoat. After the loss of the Holy Land, they continued their fight against the Turks for another 400 years, first from Rhodes and then from Malta.

Oaths of a Knight

"The knight to whom the sash is to be given shall come fully armed: and they shall ask him whether he wishes to take the sash and to be a member of the Knights of the Sash. And if he says yes, they shall say: 'You have to swear two oaths. The first is that you will serve the king all your life or will always be a vassal of the king or of one of his sons. . . . And the second oath that you have to swear is that you will love the Knights of the Sash as your brothers, and that you will never challenge a Knight of the Sash unless it is to help your father or brother. And if two Knights of the Sash quarrel or fight, you shall do everything to part them, and if you cannot part them, you shall not help either of them.' "
(From the Oath of the Knights of the Sash, *c. 1332)*

Following the failure of the Crusades, however, knights became disillusioned with the Church's ideals. They turned instead to the old books of romance, especially the tales of King Arthur and his knights. Inspired by these, they began to found new secular Orders.

The new Orders were under the patronage of either the monarch or a noble, and were inspired by the ideals of chivalry. Knights were now bound to each other and to their king by oaths of personal loyalty rather than by religion. This was a good political move. It enabled the king to raise an army more quickly, and he also knew that a knight who had sworn loyalty to him was less likely to rebel against him. These Orders still had a religious connection, however. Each was dedicated to a particular saint and celebrated that saint's feast day.

The secular Orders had rather romantic names and were sometimes dedicated to particular ideals. The Order of the White Lady on a Green Shield, for example, was sworn to protect defenseless ladies. Others included the Order of the Star, the Sash, the Golden Fleece, the Crescent, the Golden Shield, and the Falcon.

CHIVALRY

Love and War

The following lines from a contemporary account of chivalry show the close relationship between love and war in the chivalric code: "There is another category of men-at-arms who when they begin are so naive that they are unaware of the great honor that they could win through deeds of arms: nevertheless they succeed so well because they put their heart into winning the love of a lady. And they are so fortunate that their ladies themselves . . . do not want to let them tarry nor delay in any way the winning of that honor to be achieved by deeds of arms, and command them to set out and put all their efforts into winning renown and great honor." (*From Le Livre de Chevalerie, Geoffroi de Charny, mid-14th century*)

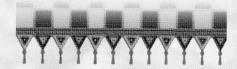

The knight's lady was sacred because she represented an earthly version of the Virgin Mary, to whom he had dedicated himself.

Chivalry was the code of behavior which transformed the knight from a fighting machine into an idealistic figure. The word itself comes from *chevalier*, the French word for "knight." It emerged in the 12th century and declined in the late Middle Ages.

The knight had to dedicate himself to carrying out brave deeds, performed unselfishly and from the noblest of motives. Everything he did was supposed to be based on trust, loyalty, and a generosity of spirit that raised the knight above common men.

One of the most important aspects of chivalry was the protection of women, who were treated almost like saints. Each knight chose a lady to whom he dedicated himself in a relationship called "courtly love." This was not like a real courtship but purely idealistic—often the lady was already married to someone else, perhaps even to the knight's lord. The knight worshiped her at a distance, hoping for her approval. Once this had been won, her inspiration gave him

courage and strength to succeed in a quest or to win a tournament. The knight also had to defend the lady's honor and write poems praising her beauty and nobility. When he fought in a tournament, he wore a token, such as her handkerchief or glove.

This celebration of chaste and honorable love was the highest ideal of chivalry, but it was also unrealistic. Medieval women were not just passive figures waiting at home in the castle. Many of them were able, wealthy women who managed estates for long periods while their husbands were away on campaign. They frequently used the men's adoration as a way of encouraging them to more civilized behavior.

Chivalry also had a place on the battlefield. There were rules about surrender, the honorable treatment of enemies, and the payment of ransoms. Knights were forbidden to bear arms against each other except in warfare. The highest honor for a knight was to have his bravery recognized by the enemy, whom he regarded as a brother in arms.

Although chivalry encouraged the performance of daring deeds, it disapproved of knights who allowed themselves to be carried away by romantic enthusiasm. In spite of this, many knights lost their lives in foolish escapades, both on the battlefield and in peacetime.

A knight receives a token from his lady before a tournament. The loss of this to his opponent, if he was defeated, was more shaming than defeat itself.

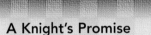

A Knight's Promise
A knight's word of honor was sacred. Froissart, chronicler of the Hundred Years' War, says that after the Battle of Crécy in 1346, the English army needed safe passage through French territory. A captured French knight, Villiers, was chosen to carry this request to the French king. He was released from prison on his solemn promise to return there when his mission was complete. Villiers was so determined to keep his word that he ignored all the king's attempts to persuade him not to return. The king, in turn, was so impressed by his honesty that he granted the English safe passage.

HERALDRY

Heraldry is the system of visual images by which noble families identify themselves. It began as a means of distinguishing one knight from another in tournaments, when they all wore full armor and helmets that covered their faces.

This Roll of Arms, known as the Herald's Roll, shows the increasing social significance of England's great families in the 1270s.

Heraldic Language

Heraldry has its own language, which is still in use today. Many of the words come from French origin. When describing colors, heralds never mention gold and silver, but "or" and "argent." Similarly, "sable" is black, "gules" red, "vert" green, "azur" blue, and "purpur" purple. They also use unusual terms for everyday images: "garb" means a wheatsheaf, "manche" is a lady's sleeve, while "lion rampant" means a lion standing on its hind legs, and "lion passant" means a lion walking sideways. The patterns also have names, such as chief, fess, chevron, bend, and bar.

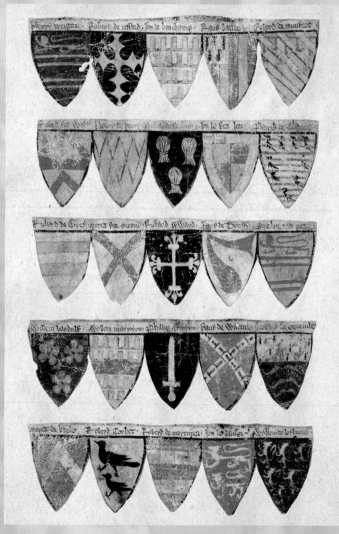

Each knight chose a symbol, or "device," and painted it on his shield on a colored background. Usually he chose an image that had special significance for his family. If they owned farmland, for example, he might choose a sheaf of corn. Animals such as lions, leopards, and dragons were also popular because they suggested bravery. The knight used this image first on his shield, but it also appeared on the surcoat he wore over his armor, on the harness of his horse, and on the banner he carried. It became his badge of identity.

Heralds were originally the men who arranged and conducted tournaments, and they were the ones responsible for keeping records of these personal devices, or "coats of arms." They compiled Rolls of Arms, listing all the arms of the great families in the land, from the king down.

These simple images soon became more complex. When families were linked by marriage their devices were combined. If an eldest son became a knight in his own right, he had to adapt his coat of arms in a way that showed his exact relationship to his father. He might repeat the same images but separate them by a geometric stripe, for example, or use a different background color.

In this way, heraldry became more than a means of identification. It was the visual expression of a knight's status and family pride. It proclaimed his ancestry and his family's noble connections in a way that was easily recognized, even by people who could not read.

The simple device that had identified the knight in a tournament became a family badge that appeared on all of his household items, on flags, and as a seal on important documents. Quite soon, the fact that a man had a coat of arms became the one important thing that established him as a knight.

The 15th-century Italian knight, Villani of Florence, chose a mythical beast, possibly a griffin, for his coat of arms.

Heraldic Images

The following speech from a verse romance about the Arthurian knight Sir Lancelot by a 12th-century French poet illustrates the variety of images used by knights on their coats of arms:

"Do you see that knight yonder with a golden band across his red shield? That is Governauz of Roberdic. And do you see that other one, who has an eagle and a dragon painted side by side on his shield? That is the son of the King of Aragon, who has come to this land in search of glory and renown. And do you see that other one beside him, who thrusts and jousts so well, bearing a shield with a leopard painted on a green ground on one part, on the other azure blue? That is Ignaures, the well-beloved, a lover himself and jovial. And he who bears the shield with the pheasants portrayed beak to beak is Coguillanz de Mautirec."
(From Le Chevalier de la Charrette, *Chrétien de Troyes, c. 1180)*

A KNIGHT'S TRAINING

The Ceremony of Knighting
The following lines describe preparations for the knighting of Geoffrey of Anjou:
"On the great day, as was required by the custom for making knights, baths were prepared. . . . After having cleansed his body, and come from the purification of bathing, [he] dressed in a linen undershirt, putting on a robe woven with gold and a surcoat of a rich purple hue: his stockings were of silk, and on his feet he wore shoes with little gold lions on them. . . . He wore a matching hauberk [mail coat] made of double mail. . . . He was shod in iron shoes, also made from double mail. To his ankles were fastened golden spurs. A shield hung from his neck, on which were golden images of lioncels [lions]. He carried an ash spear and finally a sword from the royal treasure, bearing an ancient inscription."
(*From* The Chronicles of the Counts of Anjou, c. 1100–1140)

Before they could face a real opponent, knights had to practice tilting at the quintain.

At first, only the son of a knight could become a knight himself. He began his training early, learning from his father. At the age of seven or eight, he was sent away to the home of another knight, often an uncle or his father's lord, where he began his real apprenticeship. Serving first as a page and then as a valet to his lord, he learned horsemanship and how to fight with sword, shield, and lance. He also learned to look after armor and was taught some elements of military strategy.

When he was about 15, he became a squire, a personal attendant to a particular knight. Here he probably got his first taste of action, following his lord into battle or to a tournament.

Just as important as military training, however, were civility and good manners. These set the knight apart from the common soldier. As well as learning to read and write, daily life in the great household taught him the social skills of conversation, table manners, and general courtesy. He also had to be good at singing, dancing, writing poetry, and the various games that made up the household's entertainment.

The investiture of a knight was an occasion of great spiritual significance, although the lavish ceremony often overshadowed this.

Only when he had mastered all of these skills, at the age of about 21, was a young man ready to go through the solemn ceremony which would make him a full knight. He spent the night before this ritual praying and fasting, and then he was bathed and dressed in ceremonial clothes. The highlight of the ceremony was when he was touched on the shoulder with the flat blade of a sword and given his full title. This was called "dubbing." This ceremony, the most important of a knight's life, usually took place at court or in the castle, but in times of war, squires were sometimes knighted on the battlefield. This was usually a reward for some particularly brave deed. In this way, a few boys who were not sons of knights but had shown great courage managed to attain knighthood.

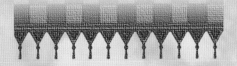

A Knight of Humble Birth
William the Marshal was the younger son of an unimportant family who made unexpected progress in society thanks to his training in knightly skills. He became famous at tournaments, where he made a fortune by defeating wealthy opponents and holding them to ransom. As a rich man, he was able to enter the king's household as tutor to his son, Henry III. He accompanied the young prince to tournaments all over Europe, and when Henry became king, William was his advisor. He eventually became the Earl of Pembroke and married a rich heiress.

A KNIGHT'S LIFE

A knight was "retained" by a local nobleman. This meant that he was one of the men the nobleman could call on when he himself was required by the king to provide soldiers for a campaign. The usual contract stated that the knight was retained for service "in peace and war, at home and abroad, and in the Holy Land."

In this 15th-century painting, a knight pays homage to his lord when he arrives at a military camp.

Hunting Skills

Almost every aspect of a knight's life prepared him for warfare. Hunting was popular not just because it was exciting but because it was a way of improving horsemanship, keeping men fit, and encouraging them to plan strategies for the chase. All of this would be useful to them in their military life. Manuals on hunting were almost as popular as books on chivalry, and all the tales of famous knights include hunting episodes. These usually involved the chase of a mysterious animal such as a stag, which led the knight into some strange adventure.

Some knights were bound to their lord as a lifelong commitment, while others were retained on a temporary basis so that a knight might serve more than one lord in his lifetime. The knight was not paid wages for his service, but he received goods and favors in return. Sir Bartholomew de Enfield, for example, was retained by the Earl of Hereford in

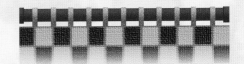

1307 and given hay for four horses, wages for three grooms, and land worth 40 marks a year. If he went to war or to a tournament, this increased to eight horses and seven grooms.

Battles and fighting were a way of life for many in medieval society, and a knight spent a good deal of his life away on campaigns. There were major foreign wars, such as the Crusades or the Hundred Years' War between England and France. In between, there was usually some lesser campaign going on against the Scots or the Welsh. At a local level, too, feuds between rival barons frequently descended into violence. The knight might be called on to serve in any of these campaigns.

Life at home was not very different from warfare. A knight served in the retinue (group of assistants) of his lord, accompanying him on pilgrimage or when he was required by the king to appear at ceremonial occasions. Most importantly, he was also retained to fight for his lord in tournaments, which demanded just as much skill as warfare.

Women also enjoyed hunting and hawking.

A knight might also be awarded the guardianship of a castle on his lord's behalf, where he had hunting rights and other benefits. At home, however, the knight enjoyed the civilizing company of women and had time to read and practice the other arts he had learned as a page.

The Perfect Knight

The English 14th-century poet Chaucer describes in these lines what he considers to be a perfect example of knighthood:

"There was a knight, a most distinguished man,
Who from the day on which he first began
To ride abroad had followed chivalry,
Truth, honor, generousness, and courtesy.
He had done nobly in his sovereign's war
And ridden into battle, no man more,
As well in Christian as in heathen [unreligious] places,
And ever honored for his noble graces. . . .
In 15 mortal battles he had been
And jousted for our faith at Tramissene
Thrice [three times] in the lists, and always killed his man. . . .
He was of sovereign value in all eyes.
And though so much distinguished, he was wise
And in his bearing modest as a maid.
He never yet a boorish [rude] thing had said
In all his life to any, come what might;
He was a true, a perfect gentle-knight."

(*From* The Canterbury Tales: General Prologue, *Geoffrey Chaucer, c. 1390s*)

A KNIGHT'S ARMOR

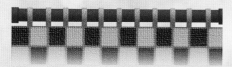

Dressing a Knight

The following lines from a poem show how complex the business of getting dressed for battle was in medieval times:
"Then they set the steel shoes on the strong man's feet,
Lapped his legs in steel with lovely greaves [lower leg armor],
Complete with knee-pieces, polished bright
And connecting at the knee with gold-knobbed hinges.
Then came the cuisses [thigh armor], which cunningly enclosed
His thighs thick of thew [muscle], and which thongs secured.
Next the hauberk [mail tunic], interlinked with argent steel rings
And resting on rich material, wrapped the warrior round.
He had polished armor on arms and elbows,
Glinting and gay, and gloves of metal,
And all the goodly gear to undergo what might betide.
With richly wrought [decorated] surcoat
And red-gold spurs to ride,
And sword of noble note
At his silken-girdled side."
(*From* Sir Gawain and the Green Knight, II, iv, *late 14th century*)

The design of armor changed considerably during the medieval period, to keep pace with new advances in weaponry. In the 12th century, the knight's body armor was a full-length hauberk, or tunic, made of tiny interlocking rings of metal known as chain mail. Under this he wore a linen shirt and breeches. The hauberk had a hood, also of mail and lined with fabric for comfort, which framed his face like a balaclava when it was pulled up. The metal helmet worn over this was more like a round cap, with a strip coming down to protect the nose, and it was attached to the hauberk by leather laces. Later in the century, hauberks were shortened to thigh-length and were worn with leggings, also made of chain mail.

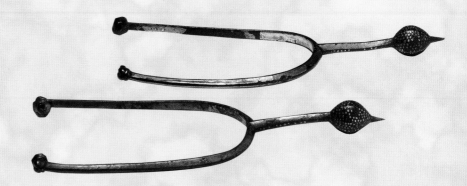

These 11th-century spurs, intended for everyday use, are very simple. Later, a knight's tournament spurs might be made of engraved gold or silver.

Although chain mail was flexible and allowed the knight to move freely, it was hard to maintain because it rusted, and the links broke easily. Also, while it gave some protection against sword strokes, it was easily pierced by arrows.

As the longbow came into use in the 13th century, chain mail gave way to plate armor. At first, knights simply fitted metal plates over their knees and elbows, but eventually the whole body was encased in metal armor, with a chain mail "aventail" around the neck to cover the vulnerable area between armor and helmet. Over his armor the knight wore a linen surcoat, on which his coat of arms appeared.

Helmets were by now generally round, either with slits for the eyes or with a visor which could be slid up and down. Attached to the feet were spurs, sharp metal points to help the knight urge on his horse. These new suits of armor gave better protection, but they could become very hot for the wearer. However, contrary to popular belief, they were not too heavy or cumbersome. A suit of plate armor weighed around 50 pounds (22 kg), and allowed flexibility of movement—essential for any knight engaged in battle.

The best armor came from Italy, Germany, and Flanders. By the 15th century, armor was sometimes elaborately engraved. Being very expensive and highly prized, it was often included in the ransom demanded when a knight was captured.

Armor changed a good deal over the centuries. The Norman knight of 1066 (left) would hardly recognize the metal-clad fighter of 1480 (right).

Spurs
Spurs carried particular symbolic significance in the knight's armory. When he was knighted, especially if this happened on the battlefield as a result of some particularly brave deed, he was said to have "won his spurs." If a knight was disgraced, the spurs were torn from his feet. In the famous Order of the Falcon, special golden spurs were awarded to knights who had been on crusade. One spur meant that he had been on campaign; two meant that he had seen action against the enemy.

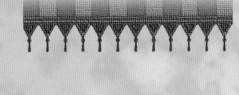

| 1066 | 1180 | 1250 | 1340 | 1380 | 1480 |

A KNIGHT AND HIS WEAPONS

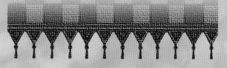

A Knight's Horse

Horses were invaluable, and the knight needed a selection of different breeds. For social riding, hunting, and traveling between battles, he rode a palfrey, a light, swift saddle-horse that could also be ridden by ladies. Only the huge war horse, or destrier, however, could carry a fully armed knight into battle. These were more than 6.5 feet (2 m) high at the withers (shoulders), heavily built, and tiring to ride. The squire rode a strong but less purebred horse known as a rouncy. Like their riders, horses often wore elaborate armor for war or tournaments, with helmets and ornamental breastplates adorned with trinkets and sometimes jewels.

In this painting of the Battle of Auray in 1364, soldiers are fighting with longbows, lances, swords, and axes.

A retained knight had to provide his own weapons. These included a sword and shield, a lance or spear, and a dagger. Tournament weapons were identical to those of real warfare, except that they were lighter and meant to be blunt, although this rule was not always obeyed.

The wooden lance, iron-tipped and up to 10 feet (3 m) long, was carried under the knight's arm and later on a swivel attached to his armor, which made it easier to aim. This was the first weapon of the knight's armory. The sword and shield were the next stage, for closer encounters. Warding off blows with his shield while slicing with his sword was the knight's greatest skill.

A squire was responsible for keeping his knight's weapons in good order, and also helped to arm him before battle.

Once dismounted, he depended on other weapons for close hand-to-hand fighting. These included a sort of spiked club called a mace, an ax, and a dagger. Many a knight, on foot and clumsy, was killed by a clever dagger stroke between the plates of his armor.

Without doubt, though, the knight's most essential weapon was his sword. There were many styles, mostly elaborate and with patterns etched into the flat blade. The best were made in Spain. A knight used the same sword throughout his life, and swords were often given names. They became as famous as the knight himself. In the old legends, Charlemagne's sword was called Joyeuse, and it was said to have magical properties, as was King Arthur's sword, Excalibur. Roland, hero of one of the early chivalric ballads, called his sword Durendal, and to prevent it from falling into the hands of the enemy, he tried to destroy it himself.

No knight would dream of using a crossbow or a longbow, which were considered to be weapons of the peasant foot soldiers. They were, in any case, impossible to handle on horseback. Nevertheless, they inflicted the most damage in battle. A single arrow from a longbow traveled at the speed of a modern rifle bullet and could fell a horse and rider.

Another weapon used against knights was the halberd, a type of spear with an extra curved blade for hooking them off their horses.

A Blessing
The following lines are a prayer for the blessing of a sword:
"Hearken, we beseech [beg] Thee, O Lord, to our prayers, and deign [consent] to bless with the right hand of Thy majesty this sword with which this Thy servant desires to be girded [equipped], that it may be a defense of churches, widows, orphans, and all Thy servants against the scourge of [trouble caused by] the pagans [non-Christians], that it may be the terror and dread of other evildoers, and that it may be just both in attack and defense."
(_From Essor de la Chevalerie, Flori, 14th century_)

KNIGHTS AT WAR

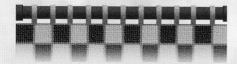

Triumph at Agincourt
The following verses are from a poem written in the early 15th century about the Battle of Agincourt, 1415:
"Our king went forth to Normandy
With grace and might of chivalry.
There God for him wrought marvellously:
Wherefore England may call and cry,
'Deo gracias'. . .
There dukes and earls, lord and baron,
Were taken and slain (killed), and that well soon,
And some were led into London
With joy and mirth and great renown."
(*From* The Agincourt Carol, *1415*)

Looting of treasure from captured towns was as common in the Hundred Years' War as in the capture of Jerusalem, shown here.

In war, a knight might face ranks of others just like himself in mounted combat or, more likely but less exciting, be in command of a battalion besieging a castle or fortified town. Victory usually depended on the capture of such places, and sieges went on for months.

Once the huge catapults had battered the walls, knights were the assault troops who scaled the ladders and stormed the citadel. Guns and gunpowder were hardly known until the 15th century, and fighting, when it happened, was mostly on a one-to-one basis. Bands of knights also raided surrounding villages or went in search of supplies, especially if a long siege had exhausted their own food stocks.

Because warfare was so commonplace, people took for granted behavior that people today would find shocking.

The siege of Antioch in 1098 lasted for eight months before the city eventually fell to the crusaders.

A captured town or castle was usually burned, its treasures looted, and innocent civilians cruelly massacred. It was the knight's responsibility to control his troops and prevent the worst of these actions, in accordance with his oaths of charity and chivalry.

If he was involved in individual combat, a knight was more fortunate. Warfare followed the rules of chivalry. For a knight from a good family, being captured was not usually a problem. He could depend on decent treatment at the enemy's hands, and he knew that a ransom would be paid by his family for his release. Although knights pretended to despise these mercenary deals, in reality, ransoms were big business, and it was a very common practice.

The adventures of knights in battle were written down by chroniclers. The Battle of Crécy in 1346, for example, was recorded by the French chronicler Froissart, and his account tells a lot about the period. However, like newspapers today, the chroniclers sometimes made sensational claims about heroic deeds. They also tended to avoid the harsh realities of war.

Every knight dreamed of the glory of dying in battle, but in reality, many died miserably from diseases such as dysentery or cholera. King Henry V, victor at Agincourt in 1415, later died like this. Others died from the treatment meant to save them. Some were weakened by blood-letting; others died as a result of agonizing battlefield surgery without anesthetic.

Chivalry in Action

The Battle of the Thirty, fought in 1351 in Brittany, is a famous example of knightly combat. English and French forces were each defending a local castle. They had been skirmishing for months to little effect. To settle things, a set-piece battle was arranged. Thirty knights on each side met exactly midway between their two castles. The battle went on for almost a whole day, with breaks for rest, and it became a series of individual duels to the death. The English commander was killed, along with many of his knights, and the rest were taken prisoner.

THE CRUSADES

For 200 years, the combined Christian armies of Europe tried to drive the Muslim rulers out of the Holy Land, and out of the city of Jerusalem in particular. These wars were known as the Crusades.

Jerusalem was sacred to Christians, Muslims, and Jews alike, but at the end of the 11th century, Christians were being prevented from going there on pilgrimage. This caused outrage in Europe, and in 1095, Pope Urban II made a speech calling for a Crusade (known as the First Crusade) to liberate the holy places. On a wave of enthusiasm, thousands of knights set off for the Holy Land, where they succeeded in capturing Jerusalem in 1099. They also established four Crusader states, which they ruled from a chain of castles.

The Children's Crusade
One of the strangest and saddest events of the religious wars was the Children's Crusade. In 1212, a 12-year-old boy named Stephen, from a village near Orléans in France, was inspired to lead a new Crusade. Believing that the innocence of children would succeed where the might of armies had failed, thousand of young boys flocked to his army. They marched to Marseilles and set sail for the Holy Land in ships supplied by generous supporters, but most were never seen again. They were tricked by the ship-owners, who took them to Algiers, North Africa, and sold them into slavery.

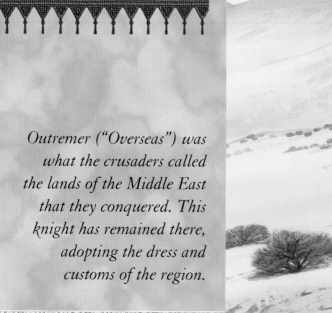

Outremer ("Overseas") was what the crusaders called the lands of the Middle East that they conquered. This knight has remained there, adopting the dress and customs of the region.

Although the clergy were forbidden to go to war or shed blood themselves, they excused it in the soldiers who went to fight on their behalf. The Pope promised that any knight who died fighting "the infidel" would have all his sins forgiven.

Knighthood became more closely associated with religion, and warfare became not just respectable but honorable. Knights wore red crosses on their tunics as a sign that they had "taken the cross"—the word "crusade" comes from the Latin word *crux*, meaning "cross." Knights began to see themselves as an international brotherhood united against a common enemy.

Many knights were inspired by genuine religious devotion, but not all crusading was idealistic. There were fortunes to be made in the Holy Land, either by seizing land, looting treasure, or holding rich enemies for ransom. Many knights returned as wealthy men. Others never returned home but stayed on as rulers of the territory they had captured. They could also behave with great cruelty. When Jerusalem was captured, the crusaders massacred all the Muslims and Jews in the city, as well as looting its treasures.

Although the First Crusade had been a triumph for the Europeans, Jerusalem was soon recaptured by the Muslims, and none of the later Christian armies was so successful. There were eight major Crusades, in which thousands of knights died. In the end, however, the great venture was a failure for the Christians, and the Holy Land remained in Muslim hands.

The knight kneeling in prayer here is thought to be King Henry III, who had taken a crusader vow.

Massacre in Jerusalem
In these lines, a French chronicler records the capture of Jerusalem in 1099:
"The Franks gloriously entered the city at noon. . . . Amid the sound of trumpets and with everything in an uproar they attacked boldly, shouting, 'God help us!' At once they raised a banner on the top of the wall. The pagans were completely terrified, for they all exchanged their former boldness for headlong flight through the narrow streets of the city. . . . Many of the Saracens who had climbed to the top of the Temple of Solomon in their flight were shot to death with arrows and fell headlong from the roof. Nearly 10,000 were beheaded in the Temple. . . . None of them were left alive. Neither women nor children were spared."
(*From* The Chronicle of Fulcher of Chartres, *1127*)

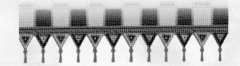

TOURNAMENTS

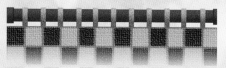

The Arthurian Tournament
The following extract describes a tournament held by King Arthur at Caerleon: "Every knight in the country who was in any way famed for his bravery wore livery [clothing] and arms showing his own distinctive color; and women of fashion often displayed the same colors. They scorned to give their love to any man who had not proved himself three times in battle. In this way the womenfolk became chaste and more virtuous, and for their love the knights were ever more daring. . . . They went out into the meadows outside the city and split up into groups. . . . The knights planned an imitation battle and competed together on horseback, while their women watched from the top of the city walls and aroused them to passionate excitement by their flirtatious behavior."
(*From* History of the Kings of Britain, *Geoffrey of Monmouth, 1136*)

Tournaments were the most important events of chivalric knighthood. They were glorious occasions, full of pageantry, and usually lasted several days.

When a tournament was announced, hundreds of knights gathered with their grooms and servants. They pitched their colorful silk tents in the nearby field. Richly dressed ladies watched from a grandstand on the opening day as the knights paraded in full armor, carrying their heraldic banners.

After the pageantry, the serious business of jousting began in the "lists." Two mounted knights armed with lances faced each other across a wooden partition. They charged, each trying to ward off the other's lance with his shield. This went on until one succeeded in knocking the other from his horse and was declared the winner.

Holding the lance steady while controlling an excited, galloping charger took all the knight's skills of horsemanship.

In some cases, the fighting continued on foot with sword and dagger until one knight surrendered and had to pay a ransom to gain his freedom. Although they were intended as entertainment, these contests were dangerous occasions, and there were many casualties. The tournament ended with a general contest involving all the knights in a ceremonial mock-battle. Most of the knights taking part in a tournament appeared as representatives of the lord by whom they were retained. However, because success depended on individual skill, tournaments also attracted a number of wandering knights—"knights-errant"—in search of a reputation and the rich prize money.

Fighting was only a part of it, however. In addition to the competing knights and the nobility, tournaments attracted crowds of ordinary folk. Horse dealers, moneylenders, minstrels, and fortune-tellers gave the event the lively air of a carnival. After the combat, knights and ladies spent hours feasting, dancing, playing games, and competing in more sedate sports, such as archery.

Tournaments were frequently organized around a theme, involving fancy dress and amateur theatricals—"King Arthur and the Round Table" was one popular theme. The craze for tournaments was so great that the nobility tried to outdo each other in staging ever more extravagant displays. Some even went bankrupt in the attempt.

A fancy-dress tournament joust between a Christian knight and a "Saracen" plays out the Crusades in the safety of England.

Mock Warfare

The tournament began as a training ground where young men could try their skills and established knights could practice and keep fit during peacetime. The 12th-century mêlée was a free-for-all mock-battle, fought over miles of open countryside and involving hundreds of knights on each side. Although the object was to capture and ransom the enemy rather than kill them, many knights were killed or badly wounded. The Church condemned these violent and chaotic episodes. Kings feared them too, because they were often a cover for the start of a real rebellion.

KNIGHTS OF MYTH AND LEGEND

The Amazons
Chivalry was not entirely a man's world, at least in legend. The Amazons were a mythical race of warrior women who supposedly lived in lands far beyond Europe. They wore armor and were as skillful as men at jousting and combat. Sometimes, wandering knights encountered these fearsome women on their travels and were challenged to battle. Frequently, they were defeated. These tales were very popular around the time of Shakespeare (16th century), and there are references to Amazons in his plays, too. Hippolyta, Queen of the Amazons, is a character in his comedy *A Midsummer Night's Dream*.

Knights were always looking to the heroes of the past for inspiration. Charlemagne and Roland, heroes of the earliest ballads, inspired the knights of the 12th century to rival their glorious deeds. Another popular figure was the Cid, a Spanish knight who rose from humble birth. His loyalty to his king even in the face of wrongful banishment made him an example to all would-be knights.

Because most of these stories were not written down until long after they were supposed to have happened, it is hard to know if they are true, and even whether the characters really existed. Saint George, for example, is the patron saint of England and of the Order of the Garter. He is often shown killing a dragon. This probably didn't really happen! But George was a real knight, although he actually came from the Middle East and not from England.

St. George's most famous exploit was rescuing a lady from a fearsome dragon.

In Britain, the most popular stories are those about King Arthur and his Knights of the Round Table. These were already old tales when Sir Thomas Malory wrote them down in the 1400s. Sir Lancelot, Galahad, Gawain, and the other knights experience wonderful adventures in their quest for the Holy Grail, a relic of Christ's crucifixion. Only Galahad, the perfect knight,

Sir Lancelot kneels before King Arthur and Queen Guinevere at the court in Camelot, the starting point for many knightly adventures.

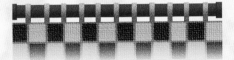

Lament for a Knight
The following lines form part of Sir Ector's lament for Lancelot, the most famous of King Arthur's Knights of the Round Table:
" 'Ah, Lancelot!' he said, 'thou were the best of all Christian knights! And now . . . there thou liest, thou who were never matched by the hand of earthly knight. And thou were the most steadfast [steady] knight that ever carried a shield! And thou were the truest friend to thy comrade that ever bestrode a horse, and thou were the truest lover, for a sinful man, that ever loved woman, and thou were the kindest man that ever struck with a sword. And thou were the goodliest [best] person that ever came among a crowd of knights, and thou was the gentlest man and the noblest that ever ate in the hall among ladies.' "
(From Le Morte d'Arthur, *Sir Thomas Malory, 1484)*

succeeds in the quest, and in the end, the fellowship of the Round Table is destroyed by Lancelot's treachery.

Equally popular in England were tales set during the Crusades. Sir Robert of Loxley, wrongly accused by the wicked Sheriff of Nottingham, becomes the outlaw Robin Hood. Hiding in Sherwood Forest, he continues to perform knightly deeds in secret until King Richard the Lionheart (Richard I) returns. Ivanhoe, created by Scottish novelist Sir Walter Scott in the early 19th century, is another knight caught up in the Crusades.

One of the last and most famous of the legendary knights is the Spaniard Don Quixote, an old man inspired by ancient tales to set off on a quest in honor of a beautiful lady. Sadly, he finds that the ideals of chivalry are long dead, and people only make fun of him.

THE END OF KNIGHTHOOD

Decline in Chivalric Values
The following extract, from a book written in about 1387, draws a sad contrast between the old ideals of the knight and the new ways of waging war:

"The way of warfare does not follow the ordinances [laws] of worthy chivalry or of the ancient custom of noble warriors who upheld justice, the widow, the orphan, and the poor. And nowadays it is the opposite that they do everywhere, and the man who does not know how to set a place on fire, to rob churches, and to usurp [seize] the rights and to imprison the priests, is not fit to carry on war. And for these reasons, the knights of today have not the glory and praise of the old champions of former times."
(*From* The Tree of Battles, *Honoré Bonet, 1387*)

By the end of the 15th century, the great tradition of knighthood was in decline. One of the main reasons for this was a change in the army itself. Instead of a brotherhood of noble knights fighting together, the army was now made up of a larger number of professional foot soldiers. These still came from the common people, but they were trained to a higher standard than the old peasant conscripts and needed only a few officers to lead them.

Foot soldiers and archers face mounted knights in battle during the Hundred Years' War.

Weapons of war had also changed. Cannons, guns, and gunpowder were now in general use, and shooting from a distance had replaced the knight's style of close-up personal combat.

Another reason for its decline was that knighthood had lost its good reputation in the eyes of ordinary men. People felt that too many men of low birth had been admitted into Orders. There were charges of drunkenness and bad behavior, which fell short of the chivalric ideal. People were disgusted, too, at

28

the way knights had returned from foreign wars with great fortunes, especially since they knew that much of the wealth had come from looted treasure.

Over the years, many unemployed knights had become mercenaries, offering their services to any army for money. Poor or disgraced knights had turned to robbery. Throughout Europe, "free companies" of wandering knights roamed the countryside, terrorizing the very people they had sworn to protect. Poets of the time had begun to make fun of the ideals of chivalry, instead of glorifying its heroes. All this helped to hasten the end of knighthood.

As knighthood lost its chivalric and military glamor, however, it became more important in the social world. Knights were the third most important social class, after the king and the nobility. They made up juries and served in local government. In England, they formed the basis of the House of Commons.

A knighthood was still a great prize, but it was now little more than an honorary title handed out by the king. Knighthood as a way of life to which all young men aspired was gone forever.

Revival of Interest

Three hundred years later, the 19th century saw a wave of nostalgia for all things medieval. Victorian writers such as Alfred, Lord Tennyson and William Morris retold the tales of King Arthur, and the Pre-Raphaelite artists painted scenes from these and other chivalric romances. The Earl of Eglinton, however, went one better and staged a tournament, complete with jousting. The Eglinton Tournament of 1839 was a protest against the lack of traditional pageantry at the recent coronation of Queen Victoria. Everyone was in medieval dress, the "knights" fought in full armor, a jester entertained, and the "Queen of Beauty" presided over the occasion. It ended with a magnificent ball and banquet. And, just like the old tournaments, it cost the earl a fortune.

The artist Edward Burne-Jones made the romantic knightly tales popular all over again in the 19th century. This tapestry shows knights setting off on the quest for the Holy Grail.

TIMELINE

500–843	First mounted "knights" appear in Frankish kingdom of France and Germany.
c. 537	Death of Arthur, King of the Britons.
773–804	Campaigns of Charlemagne and his knights.
1066	England is conquered by the Normans.
1095	Pope Urban II calls for the First Crusade.
1099	Jerusalem captured by knights of the First Crusade.
1120	Foundation of the Knights Templar.
1130	Pope Urban II bans tournaments.
1147–49	The Second Crusade.
1187	Jerusalem recaptured by the Muslim leader Saladin. The Third Crusade.
1190	Order of Teutonic Knights founded in Germany.
1204	Knights of the Fourth Crusade conquer Constantinople and set up a Latin empire.
1212	The Children's Crusade.
1291	Capture of Acre and loss of Holy Land by Christians.
1307–14	Knights Templar investigated for heresy and eventually disbanded.
1307–27	Reign of Edward II, under whom tournaments became lavish occasions.
1337–1453	The Hundred Years' War between England and France.
1347	The Order of the Garter founded by Edward III at a tournament at Windsor.
c. 1350	Guns and other firearms begin to feature in battle.
1415	Battle of Agincourt: French defeated by English under Henry V.
1621	Last official tournament in England.

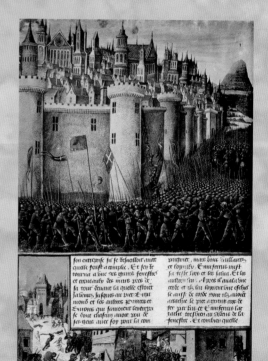

GLOSSARY AND FURTHER INFORMATION

allegiance Loyal obedience.

argent Silver.

balaclava A hood that covers the face, with holes for eyes and mouth.

ballad A romantic story told in verse.

cholera A disease caused by dirty water.

chronicler Someone who records events.

citadel Fortress.

clergy Churchmen.

conscript Someone called for compulsory military service.

contemplative A monk or nun dedicated to religious study.

Crusades Wars between Christians and Muslims.

cuisses Armor covering the thighs.

destrier A heavy war horse.

device Ornamental picture.

dysentery Disease causing diarrhea.

feud Long-standing rivalry between two people.

Grail The bowl used by Jesus at the Last Supper.

greaves Lower-leg armor.

halberd A spear with a hook to pull a knight off his horse.

hauberk A long mail coat.

idealistic Aiming at the highest good.

infidel Medieval Christians' name for Muslims, literally "those of no faith."

lists Barriers enclosing the tournament field.

mace A spiked club.

mêlée A mock battle.

mercenary A hired soldier.

pageantry Ceremonial display.

palfrey A light horse used for traveling.

patronage Favor.

pillage To rob using violence.

ransom Money paid for the release of a prisoner.

rebellion Fight against one's own lord or king.

rouncy A squire's horse.

Saracen A Muslim, or any Arab.

secular Not based on religion.

skirmish Brief military fight.

squire Knight's personal attendant.

surcoat Tunic worn on top of mail.

valet Manservant.

vassal Loyal subject.

visor Hinged flap of helmet which covers the eyes.

RECOMMENDED READING

Byam, Michele. *Arms and Armor.* New York: DK Publishing, 2000.

Corrick, James A. *Life of a Medieval Knight.* New York: Gale Group, 2000.

Gravett, Christopher. *Knight.* New York: DK Publishing, 2000.

Langley, Andrew. *Medieval Life.* New York: DK Publishing, 2000.

Oakeshott, Ewart. *A Knight and His Armor.* Chester Springs, Pa.: Dufour Editions, 1999.

———. *A Knight and His Weapons.* Chester Springs, Pa.: Dufour Editions, 1997.

Scott, Walter. *Ivanhoe.* New York: Random House, 2001.

RECOMMENDED WEB SITES

http://www.metmuseum.org/explore/knights/title.html

http://www.channel4.com/history/microsites/H/history/guide12/index.html

http://www.mnsu.edu/emuseum/history/middleages

http://www.cybrary.org/medieval.htm

http://www.knightsandarmor.com/index.htm

INDEX